*sparkteach

TEACHING THE CLASSICS TO TODAY'S STUDENTS

The Great Gatsby

F. SCOTT FITZGERALD

*sparknotes FOR TEACHERS™

*sparkteach

ISBN 978-1-4114-8013-1

Distributed in Canada by Sterling Publishing Co., Inc.
C/o Canadian Manda Group, 664 Annette Street
Toronto, Ontario M6S 2C8, Canada
Distributed in the United Kingdom by GMC Distribution Services
Castle Place, 166 High Street, Lewes, East Sussex BN7 1XU, England
Distributed in Australia by NewSouth Books
University of New South Wales, Sydney, NSW 2052, Australia

For information about custom editions, special sales, and premium
and corporate purchases, please contact Sterling Special Sales
at 800-805-5489 or specialsales@sterlingpublishing.com.

Manufactured in Canada

2 4 6 8 10 9 7 5 3 1

sparkteach.com
sparknotes.com
sterlingpublishing.com

Cover design by Elizabeth Mihaltse Lindy
Cover and title page illustration by MUTI
Interior design by Kevin Ullrich
Image credits: iStock/Getty Images Plus/filborg: 14,15;
Library of Congress: 25, 26 bottom; Wellcome Collection: 26 top

Contents

PART 1
Welcome to SparkTeach!

SparkTeach is a unique set of teaching guides and lesson plans designed to help make classic literature engaging and relevant to today's students.

We asked teachers about the biggest challenges they face in their English classes, and their answer was clear: "We need to engage our students, spark their interest in literature, and make our lessons relevant." That's why we developed SparkTeach, customizable materials including teaching frameworks, lessons, in-class worksheets, and more for the most popular titles taught today!

The following pages provide you with helpful tips for lesson planning and classroom management, an explanation of each component, including a detailed description of a "Real-Life Lens Lesson"; an explanation of the role of the ELA Common Core State Standards in the program; and guidelines for student assessment.

SparkTeach materials are easily customizable and can be adapted for many different learning styles. We encourage you to utilize the lessons as best fits your classroom's needs.

Tips for Class Planning and Management

Here are some tips for planning and managing your class as students work their way through a SparkTeach unit. To maximize student learning and engagement:

1. Preview SparkTeach Materials

Review all the materials available for a text. Decide which worksheets you will use based on student needs. You may choose materials to match a particular text in your curriculum, or you may assign a text after being inspired by a specific Real-Life Lens Lesson.

2. Gather Your Materials

Once you've selected the components you'll need, preview each lesson and then download and print all of the chosen worksheets. Be sure to print out enough copies for each student and one copy for yourself to use as reference. Hand out all worksheets needed prior to reading, such as Contextual Support Handouts, as these promote student comprehension.

If the Real-Life Lens Lesson requires a specific film, make sure to have the film on hand to show the class. If specific scene timestamps are provided, preview the scenes so that you will feel prepared to answer students' questions.

Review the Midpoint Activities and Final Project options in the Real-Life Lens Lesson. Will you need specific equipment such as a video recorder or a printer for students to complete a project? Be sure your students will have access to the tools they'll need to complete their work.

3. Set Your Schedule

Once you've chosen a Real-Life Lens Lesson, read it through before starting. Choose your start, midpoint, and end dates to keep on schedule. Each framework should take multiple class periods to complete; plan each activity and project accordingly. Will students need access to the school library or the internet to conduct research for their final projects? If so, be sure to schedule time for student research, review, and revision.

4. Preview Real-Life Links

Read, watch, or listen to each of the Real-Life Links. Decide which resources will engage your students the most. Prepare a few questions to use to ignite student thinking, guide quick written responses, and initiate class discussion.

5. Monitor Student Progress and Comprehension

Routinely schedule one-on-one meetings with students to check their comprehension and progress throughout reading. During group work or discussions, circulate around the room to monitor student collaboration and communication and to gently guide discussions back on topic, if necessary. Recording your observations and assessments will enable you to note individual and whole-class progress as work continues.

6. Let Students Shine

Schedule plenty of time for all students to present their final projects. They have worked hard all month, and showing off their finished work boosts confidence and allows students to see the unique and creative ways their peers interpreted and approached a similar topic.

7. Personalize Content

Real-Life Lens Lessons are designed to ensure students engage with each text in a meaningful way. Lenses are specially chosen to help students connect with even the most challenging texts on a personal level. As you progress through the materials, look for ways to help students relate the text to their own lives. Notice what excites them and tailor your lessons accordingly.

What's Included in SparkTeach?

Real-Life Lens Lessons

The Real-Life Lens Lesson is a unit that focuses on a specific text over multiple class periods. The driving force behind each unit is the lens, a carefully selected theme through which students view the text. This lens provides students with a relatable point of entry, A thorough explanation of each feature in a Real-Life Lens Lesson is detailed in the next section beginning on page 8. Each Real-Life Lens Lesson includes several downloadable worksheets and assessment materials to round out the unit.

Reading Skills Worksheets

Each set of teaching materials features multiple Reading Skills Worksheets designed to help develop the ELA reading skills outlined in the Common Core State Standards. Worksheets engage students in a variety of activities that deepen understanding of both the skill and the featured text. Each worksheet is printable.

Vocabulary Builders

Each set of teaching materials also includes at least one Vocabulary Builder based on the specific language found in the text. You can pass out the builder prior to starting the text and refer to it as students read to ensure comprehension. Other builders ask students to engage with the vocabulary through graphic organizers, charts, or other activities. Each builder is printable.

Contextual Support Handouts

To aid comprehension, each set of teaching materials features at least one Contextual Support handout to provide information to students about topics relevant to the text. Student comprehension is hindered if historical or background information is unknown or not clear. We developed these handouts to arm students with the information they'll need to better understand each text.

What Makes Real-Life Lens Lessons Unique?

Real-Life Lens Lessons, the hub of SparkTeach materials, set this literature program apart. Each Real-Life Lens Lesson is thoughtfully designed to help students view the text—even older or more challenging works—through a relatable lens, that enables students to connect with the text in a meaningful way. A powerful teaching tool, each teacher-facing Real-Life Lens Lesson provides a framework for organizing and executing a unit over multiple class periods that focuses on a particular work of literature. Each element found in a Real-Life Lens Lesson is listed and described below.

1. The Lens

The lens is the heart of each Real-Life Lens Lesson. The lens shapes classroom discussions, student analysis, and all lesson activities and projects. The lens invites students to explore the text in a way that connects the content with their own lives—their experiences, concerns, interests, and aspirations.

Introduce the Lens Through Real-Life Links

- Each Real-Life Lens Lesson features several Real-Life Links including online articles, podcasts, videos, and surveys.

- Real-Life Links are meant to be shared with students prior to or during reading.

- After students read, listen to, or watch the Real-Life Links, but before reading of the text begins, the class participates in an activity designed to introduce the lens to students in a meaningful way.

2. Big Idea Questions

- The Big Idea Questions are overarching questions that provide students with a base from which to start thinking about the text. For example: "What does it mean to achieve the American Dream?" (See page 15.)

- Students are encouraged to return to these questions as they read and note how their answers to the questions change over the course of the unit.

3. Driving Questions

In addition to the Big Idea Questions, each Real-Life Lens Lesson contains a number of Driving Questions. Unlike the Big Idea Questions, Driving Questions are more specific in their focus and are designed to guide student exploration of the text, as related to the lens. Some examples of Driving Questions featured in *The Great Gatsby* include:

- How is Gatsby's love for Daisy a metaphor for the American Dream?

- What is each character's motivation for achieving the American Dream?

- Has Gatsby achieved the American Dream before the end of the novel?

4. Differentiated Instruction

- To ensure all students can access learning, we have provided differentiated instruction for all Midpoint Activities and final projects.

- Suggestions for increasing and/or decreasing the difficulty of each activity and project are found throughout each Real-Life Lens Lesson.

5. Midpoint Activities

- Two engaging Midpoint Activities are featured to ensure student comprehension of the text and give you an opportunity to assess learning.

- These activities encourage students to consolidate their understanding of the text so far and challenge them to use that understanding to make predictions about the rest of the text and analyze what they know of the plot, characters, or theme.

6. Paired Text Recommendations

- Our list of paired text recommendations suggests contemporary novels you can pair with the classic novel you're teaching.

- Students can connect to passages from multiple novels by comparing, contrasting, and analyzing the works side by side.

7. Final Projects

- Each Real-Life Lens Lesson presents students with two options for final projects that encapsulate what they have learned about the text as seen through the lens.

- Students are invited to choose the project that excites them the most at the beginning of the unit and to keep this project in mind as they read.

- These dynamic projects are designed to provide opportunities for students to demonstrate their mastery of the text in creative and fun ways.

- Examples of projects include creating a multimedia presentation or video, rewriting and performing a scene from the text, and participating in a formal debate on a specific issue.

8. Supporting Worksheets and Graphic Organizers

- Each Real-Life Lens Lesson offers several printable worksheets, including a **Driving Questions Worksheet, located on page 41,** on which students can record answers as they read, and graphic organizers to support student learning.

- To save you time and help students understand how to tackle each task, each worksheet includes scaffolded directions and a sample student response if necessary.

9. Student and Teacher Reflection Worksheets

- The **Student Reflection Worksheet, located on page 50,** encourages students to assess their strengths, weaknesses, and level of engagement throughout the Real-Life Lens Lesson.

- Self-assessment cultivates confidence, as students note how they worked through challenges; nurtures good study habits; and encourages students to take responsibility for their own learning.

- The **Teacher Reflection Worksheet, located on page 51,** allows you to evaluate what elements of the unit students found the most engaging, where they seemed to struggle, and what approaches or elements worked the best for you and your class.

SparkTeach and the Common Core State Standards

Every component included in SparkTeach was developed to ensure broad coverage of the ELA Common Core State Standards. Materials were designed to provide multiple opportunities for your students to address a wide variety of Reading Literature, Speaking and Listening, Writing, and Language standards.

Each standard addressed by an activity, discussion, or project is listed for easy reference so that you can track which standards each lesson or worksheet covers.

Guidelines for Student Assessment

Each set of SparkTeach materials provides extensive assessment opportunities, including a **Rubric for Student Assessment, a Student Reflection Worksheet, and a Teacher Reflection Worksheet (see pages 45–51).** Use these assets, along with lesson-specific assessment advice within each Real-Life Lens Lesson, to successfully gauge student learning.

Worksheet Assessment

Many Reading Skills Worksheets and Vocabulary Builders may be scored in a traditional fashion. To make grading easier and faster, we have provided full answer keys for worksheets that contain clear correct or incorrect answers and sample student answers for worksheets that require more subjective, open-ended answers.

Real-Life Lens Lesson Assessment

Each Real-Life Lens Lesson offers opportunities for informal, formal, and self-assessment. Performance assessment involves observing student collaboration, while formal assessment entails grading a writing assignment, worksheet, or final project.

PART 2

SparkTeach
The Great Gatsby
Lesson Plan

Real-Life Lens Lesson

The American Dream

Use this Real-Life Lens Lesson to help students dive deep into *The Great Gatsby* by F. Scott Fitzgerald and examine the novel's themes, actions, and characters through the lens of the American Dream. How does the American Dream relate to *The Great Gatsby*? Do any of the characters in the novel actually achieve the American Dream? Is achieving the American Dream even possible?

Materials

   The Great Gatsby by F. Scott Fitzgerald

Worksheets: Driving Questions, page 41

Greed in *The Great Gatsby*, page 43

Introduce the Lens

To activate students' thinking, choose one or two of the following Real-Life Links to use in an engagement activity. Have students read or watch and discuss the content. Encourage students to jot down notes, or record class notes on the board for future reference.

Real-Life Links: The American Dream Explored

What Is the American Dream? The History That Made It Possible
This article from *The Balance* defines the American Dream, explains the origin of the phrase, and describes the conditions that originally made this dream the ultimate goal for Americans.

https://www.thebalance.com/what-is-the-american-dream-quotes-and-history-3306009

The Transformation of the "American Dream"
In this article from the *New York Times*, the author explains what the American Dream means today as opposed to what it meant when the term was first coined, as well as how the promise of the American Dream drives our economy and government policy.

https://www.nytimes.com/2017/08/04/upshot/the-transformation-of-the-american-dream.html

Greed: The Ultimate Addiction

This essay from *Psychology Today* describes how the desire for wealth and material goods can be as dangerous as any other addiction.

https://www.psychologytoday.com/us/blog/evolution-the-self/201210/greed-the-ultimate-addiction

Defining the American Dream

In this video from the *New York Times*, New Yorkers talk about what the American Dream means to them in the aftermath of the 2008 financial crisis.

https://www.nytimes.com/video/us/1194840031120/defining-the-american-dream.html

Pleasantville

In the movie *Pleasantville*, two teenagers in the 1990s wake up to find themselves in the seemingly ideal black-and-white town of Pleasantville in the 1950s. However, they soon realize that what we tend to think of as perfection does not always lead to happiness.

https://www.youtube.com/watch?v=4dceBTg2S5k

Pose the Following Big Idea Questions to the Class:

What does it mean to achieve the American Dream?

How has the promise of the American Dream shaped the world today?

Engagement Activity

- Have students write quick initial answers to the questions.

- Discuss the questions either as a class or in small groups. Prompt students to discuss whether achieving the American Dream means having security and the basic needs in life or having as much wealth as possible, as depicted in *The Great Gatsby*.

- Encourage students to discuss how the idea of the American Dream has changed since the 1920s as well as how this concept may have stayed the same.

- Following discussion, give students time to revise their initial responses and ask volunteers to share what they wrote with the class.

CCSS: SL.11-12.1

Introduce the Driving Questions

Begin by having students write their own questions about the lesson topic. Encourage them to think about what they already know about the American Dream and what they're interested in exploring further.

Hand out the **Driving Questions Worksheet, located on page 41**. Review the questions as a class. Students should enter initial answers to the questions as they read *The Great Gatsby*. They will revisit the questions and revise their answers following the lesson activities, classroom discussion, and the completion of the text. Remind students to support their responses with text evidence.

Integrate the Driving Questions into your classroom discussions. Use them to help guide students' thinking about the Big Idea Questions.

1. What does the American Dream mean to each character in the novel?
2. How do various characters in the novel try to achieve the American Dream?
3. How is Gatsby's love for Daisy a metaphor for the American Dream?
4. How has the country changed since the days of Gatsby and Nick?
5. What is each character's motivation for achieving the American Dream?
6. Has Gatsby achieved the American Dream before the end of the novel?
7. How is the green light on Daisy's dock relevant to the American Dream?

CCSS: RL.11-12.1, W.11-12.4

Introduce the "Through the Lens" Activity

Activity: Exploring a Personal Experience

In this activity, ask students to write a few paragraphs about a time they wanted something that they couldn't have. (If students are uncomfortable writing about their own experiences, have them write about someone they know or about a character in a story or film.) Provide examples to provoke students' thinking, such as not being cast in a play, not making it onto a team, or not going somewhere far away that they wanted to visit. In their paragraphs, students should explain what it was they wanted or wanted to do, why they couldn't have it, and how the experience made them feel.

Pair students and have partners share their paragraphs. Encourage pairs to return to the Big Idea Questions and consider if and how their personal experiences informed their initial answers.

Invite three or four students to share their paragraphs with the class. Prompt whole-class discussion with questions such as: *How do you react to not getting what you want? Do you keep trying or make peace with your situation? How do your initial expectations affect your feelings when you do not get something you want?*

Before moving on, explain that students will explore how the idea of the American Dream affects the way people feel and act when they do not get everything the American Dream promises.

CCSS: W.11-12.3

Differentiated Instruction

This activity can be modified to help all students access learning.

Decrease Difficulty

Present a relatable scenario to students and ask how they would feel in a situation when they did not get what they want. For example, ask how they would feel if they wanted to buy something but could not afford it. Proceed with discussion as outlined above.

Increase Difficulty

Instead of writing about personal experiences, have students write a short essay about what might happen to people who consistently do not get what they want. Ask two or three students to read their essays to the class and proceed with discussion as outlined above.

Introduce the Final Project

Before moving on, introduce the final projects to the class (see pages 20–21). Have students choose the project they will complete and encourage them to keep their project in mind as they read the text. Facilitate the formation of project groups if necessary.

Assign the Midpoint Activities

Activity 1: Greed

Students will explore the theme of greed in *The Great Gatsby* by writing about how this theme relates to each character. Hand out the **Greed in *The Great Gatsby* Worksheet, located on page 43.** Students will:

- complete a graphic organizer that has each character's name to indicate whether each character is greedy. If a character is greedy, students should explain what motivates that greed.
- share their answers with the class and discuss with each other which characters most exemplify the theme of greed.

RL.11-12.2

Differentiated Instruction

Decrease Difficulty

Choose one main character from the novel and ask students if they think that character exhibits signs of greed. Proceed with discussion as outlined above.

Increase Difficulty

Have students select two characters from the worksheet who they think are greedy and write an essay comparing and contrasting what motivates their greed.

Activity 2: Reverse Point of View

Students will think about the events of the novel thus far from the perspective of a character other than Nick. Students will:

- choose one of the main characters in the novel who is not Nick.

- pick a main event that has occurred in the novel so far. Write about that event from the point of view of their chosen character.

- have a whole-class discussion about how looking at the story from a different perspective affects how they think about the characters, including Nick.

RL.11-12.6, SL.11-12.4, W.11-12.3

Differentiated Instruction

Decrease Difficulty

Ask students about one character who is not Nick and have them discuss how they think that character feels about a specific event in the novel. Proceed with discussion as outlined above.

Increase Difficulty

Have students choose one major event that has occurred in the novel so far and write about the event from the perspective of three characters who are not Nick. Have pairs discuss what the different perspectives tell them about the characters.

Paired Text Recommendations

Encourage students to read passages from contemporary works that similarly feature the theme of the American Dream. In pairing multiple texts with similar themes, students are challenged to look beyond the book they're studying and find new ways to connect to the themes. Here are some books you can pair with *The Great Gatsby*:

- *We Were Liars* by E. Lockhart

- *Between the World and Me* by Ta-Nehisi Coates

- *Behold the Dreamers* by Imbolo Mbue

Final Projects

Students will work on their final projects after they have finished reading *The Great Gatsby*. Project 1 can be completed in groups, while Project 2 can be completed individually.

> CCSS: W.11-12.1, W.11-12.2, W.11-12.4, W.11-12.9, SL.11-12.1, SL.11-12.2, SL.11-12.3, SL.11-12.4

Final Project 1: Did Gatsby Achieve the American Dream?

Students will first debate whether Gatsby actually achieved the American Dream and then use the evidence provided by both sides of the debate to write a persuasive essay. For the debate, organize students into small groups. Students will:

- take a position of "yes" or "no" on whether Gatsby achieved the American Dream

- work together to develop their argument, being sure to include supporting text evidence from the novel and background information from the companion resources presented at the beginning of the Lens Lesson.

- produce a rebuttal against the counterclaim.

- debate a group that has the opposite position. Students not debating can take notes on ideas for their persuasive essay.

After the debate, students will use the evidence gathered to write a persuasive essay that proves whether or not Gatsby achieved the American Dream.

Differentiated Instruction

Decrease Difficulty

Rather than a formal debate, students can have a group discussion about whether Gatsby achieved the American Dream.

Increase Difficulty

Have students work individually rather than in groups and debate one other student with an opposing position.

Final Project 2: Gatsby as a Metaphor

Students will work individually to write an essay explaining how Gatsby's arc is similar to that of the American economy in the 1920s. Students will:

- review the text and note the key events in Gatsby's life as well as what brought him to each event.

- research the U.S. economy in the 1920s, including the events that led up to the Great Depression.

- write an essay explaining how Gatsby is a metaphor for the rise and fall of the American Dream in the 1920s, including how his death symbolizes the Great Depression.

Differentiated Instruction

Decrease Difficulty

Students can list ways in which Gatsby's life symbolizes the American economy.

Increase Difficulty

Have students develop two timelines, one showing the events leading up to the Great Depression and one showing the major events of Gatsby's life, to accompany their essays.

Assess the Assignments

Use the **Rubric for Student Assessment, located on page 46,** to evaluate student work on the lesson assignments.

Distribute the **Student Reflection Worksheet, located on page 50.** Guide students through the self-assessment and reflection questions.

Complete the **Teacher Reflection Worksheet, located on page 51.** Record which elements of the lesson plan worked well for your class and which elements you might revise for future classes.

PART 3

Worksheets and Handouts

The American Economy in the 1920s

Overview

While most students have heard of the Great Depression, many may not be familiar with other important historical and cultural changes happening in the United States during the era in which *The Great Gatsby* is set. This handout gives students important background information about the economy after World War I, the effects of prohibition, the new emphasis on consumerism, and the events leading up to the Great Depression. Use this handout to spark discussion and debate in your classroom, and allow students to express personal experiences related to the issues described.

RL.11-12.9 Demonstrate knowledge of eighteenth-, nineteenth-, and early twentieth-century foundational works of American literature, including how two or more texts from the same period treat similar themes or topics.

How World War I Affected the Economy

World War I broke out on June 28, 1914, when Austria-Hungary declared war on Serbia following the assassination of Austria-Hungary's Archduke Franz Ferdinand. While several European countries joined the war, the United States remained neutral until 1917. At the beginning of the war, the United States was in a recession, or period of economic decline. As the United States was not participating in the war, other countries relied on the United States to manufacture materials needed for the war. This fact not only contributed to the U.S. economy but also caused factories to increase efficiency by using assembly lines, which would continue to be used for mass production throughout the 1920s..

Prohibition

In January 1919, the U.S. Congress ratified the Eighteenth Amendment, which prohibited the manufacture and sale of alcoholic beverages. The amendment took effect in January 1920 and remained in place until it was repealed in 1933. The amendment was supported and brought about by members of the temperance movement, who promoted abstaining from liquor entirely. However, many other people used this opportunity to make money by bootlegging (making liquor illegally) and running speakeasies (establishments where people could drink liquor in secret). This way of doing business led to a great deal of criminal activity and turf wars between gangs. As evidenced in *The Great Gatsby*, the ban on alcohol did little to prevent people from acquiring and drinking alcohol in great quantities if they wanted to.

Consumerism

With a booming economy and plethora of emerging technology, the 1920s was the first era of consumerism. New inventions that were affordable for many families, such as vacuum cleaners and irons, made household work easier, which in turn allowed more leisure time for families. The advertising industry also took advantage of this new consumerist mindset, pushing products in newspapers and magazines as well as on the radio. People were more willing to buy on credit as opposed to being wary of going into debt. And with Henry Ford's cars being mass-produced, automobiles were suddenly no longer a luxury. These circumstances made people like Gatsby and the Buchanans eager to show off their wealth rather than hide it.

The Events That Led to the Great Depression

While many people, similar to those in *The Great Gatsby*, enjoyed unprecedented wealth throughout the 1920s, they did not do so without eventual consequence. People of every social class invested their savings in the stock market throughout the twenties, causing the stock market to expand very quickly. However, as wages began to stagnate and people felt the burden of debt they had taken on, consumer spending slowed down while stock prices rose. Finally, in October 1929, investors began selling and trading overpriced shares that ended up being completely worthless. The stock market crashed, plummeting the U.S. economy into a depression that would last nearly ten years.

What Words Tell Us about Characters

Overview

Authors carefully select the words they to describe characters, as each word reveals a facet of his or her personality. Use this handout to support student comprehension as they read *The Great Gatsby*. Review the contents of the chart as a class. Encourage students to refer back to this worksheet as necessary as they read the text. You can also have students add to the chart as or after they read, finding their own examples of character descriptions.

RL.11-12.4 Determine the meaning of words and phrases as they are used in the text, including figurative and connotative meanings; analyze the impact of specific word choices on meaning and tone, including words with multiple meanings or language that is particularly fresh, engaging, or beautiful.

What Words Tell Us about Characters

When describing characters, authors carefully choose words with specific connotations to help readers imagine characters as accurately as possible. For example, one of Fitzgerald's first descriptions of Tom Buchanan is:

> **"His speaking voice, a gruff husky tenor, added to the impression of fractiousness he conveyed."**

The word *fractiousness* means "having the quality of being easily angered." Along with the description of Tom's rough voice, readers can easily picture a rather frightening, short-tempered man. The word *fractious* sounds stronger and more intimidating than *irritable* or *grumpy*, which are words with similar definitions but weaker connotations. This chart shows other examples of how Fitzgerald uses words with precise meanings to describe characters

Character	Word or Phrase	What the Word or Phrase Tells Us
Jay Gatsby	punctilious	*Punctilious* means "showing great attention to details or correct behavior." Gatsby did not come from a wealthy family, even though he pretends he did, and so he is overly concerned with proper etiquette. However, it is this careful attention to detail that makes people question his background.
Daisy Buchanan	tense gayety	While the words in this phrase seem to contradict each other—with *tense* meaning "rigid or nervous" and *gayety* meaning "cheerfulness"—both words work together to describe Daisy perfectly. Although she puts on airs of being lighthearted, she is in a loveless marriage, and there is something inside her that stops her from being truly happy.
Myrtle Wilson	hauteur	*Hauteur* is "pride in a way that is disdainful of others." Even though Myrtle has a modest life, she is desperate to climb the social ladder and so acts as if she is of a higher class than she actually is. The word *hauteur* shows the arrogance that is part of her act as well as her disgust with people who are not wealthy.
Jordan Baker	contemptuous	*Contemptuous* means "showing scorn or disrespect toward others," and it is used to describe Jordan several times in the novel. We see Jordan as a contrast to Daisy, as Jordan is a cynical "new woman" of the 1920s, skeptical and distrustful of others.

How Setting Affects Theme

Overview

Examining the setting helps students deepen their understanding of a text. Students will use this worksheet to explore how an event's setting can be as significant as the event itself. Hand out the worksheet before students begin reading the novel. Have students fill out the graphic organizer as they read, naming major events that happen in each place. When students finish reading, have them complete the second half of the worksheet, explaining why each specific setting was important to the related event.

RL.11-12.3 Analyze the impact of the author's choices regarding how to develop and relate elements of a story or drama (e.g., where a story is set, how the action is ordered, how the characters are introduced and developed).

How Setting Affects Theme

While what happens in a scene is obviously important, where and when the action is set can give a scene deeper meaning. Complete this graphic organizer by writing the main events that take place in each setting in *The Great Gatsby*.

Part 1: Fill out the chart as you read.

Setting	Main Events
West Egg	Gatsby throws wild parties.
East Egg	Nick visits the Buchanans.
New York City	
The Valley of Ashes	

Part 2: Explain the importance of each setting.

Explain why Fitzgerald chose to set certain scenes in each place and how the events in each particular setting contribute to the themes of the novel.

West Egg

East Egg

New York City

The Valley of Ashes

Marriage

Overview

Comparing and contrasting characters, events, and themes helps students discover larger truths in a text. Students will use this worksheet to track the progression of two marriages throughout *The Great Gatsby*: the marriage of Tom and Daisy Buchanan and the marriage of George and Myrtle Wilson. Students will then write about how the novel explores the theme of marriage.

RL.11-12.2 Determine two or more themes or central ideas of a text and analyze their development over the course of the text, including how they interact and build on one another to produce a complex account; provide an objective summary of the text.

Marriage

Two marriages are explored in *The Great Gatsby*: the marriage between Tom and Daisy Buchanan and the marriage between George and Myrtle Wilson. Explore the progression of each relationship, and then write about what this information tells you about marriage as a theme in *The Great Gatsby*.

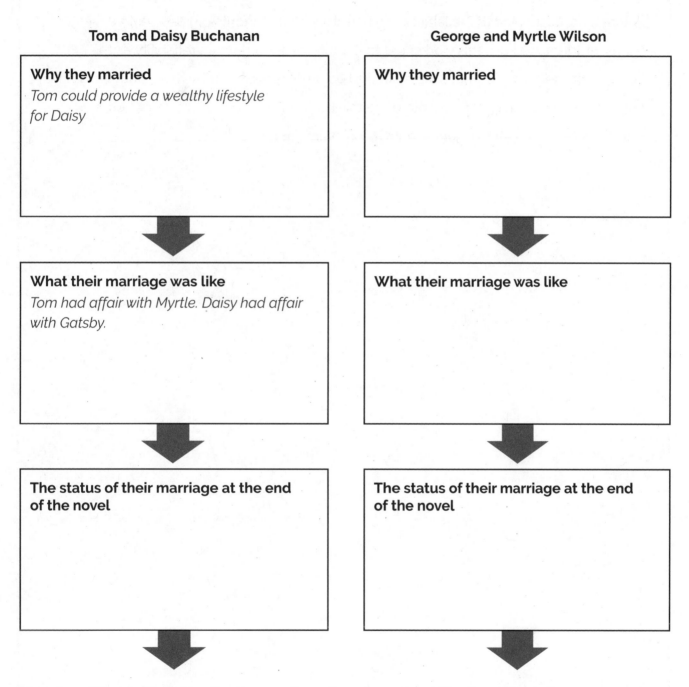

Tom and Daisy Buchanan

Why they married
Tom could provide a wealthy lifestyle for Daisy

What their marriage was like
Tom had affair with Myrtle. Daisy had affair with Gatsby.

The status of their marriage at the end of the novel

George and Myrtle Wilson

Why they married

What their marriage was like

The status of their marriage at the end of the novel

How does Fitzgerald explore the theme of marriage throughout *The Great Gatsby*?

Nick as the Narrator

Overview

Not every narrator provides clear, honest, and unbiased accounts of other characters and events. Examining the reliability of a narrator helps students dig deeper into a text's truths. Students will use this worksheet to explore Nick Carraway's reliability as the narrator. Students can complete the second column as or after they read. Once they have finished the novel, they can complete the third column. Discuss as a class whether Nick is truly as free from making judgments as he claims to be.

RL.11-12.6 Analyze a case in which grasping a point of view requires distinguishing what is directly stated in a text from what is really meant (e.g., satire, sarcasm, irony, or understatement).

Nick as the Narrator

From the beginning of the novel, Nick Carraway assures readers that he is unfailingly honest and does not make judgments about other people. However, as his is the only point of view readers actually experience, readers cannot know if Nick is truly a reliable narrator. Complete the chart by writing words Nick uses to describe the novel's characters, including himself, as well as what these descriptions reveal about Nick's opinion of each character.

Character	How Nick Describes the Character	Nick's Opinion of the Character
Jay Gatsby	having a smile with eternal reassurance, punctilious, impatient, proud of his house	While Nick disapproves of wealth and debauchery, he sees Gatsby as innocent and hopeful and ultimately too good for those he aspires to be like.
Nick Carraway		
Daisy Buchanan		
Tom Buchanan		
Jordan Baker		
Myrtle Wilson		
George Wilson		

Whom Does Daisy Love?

Overview

Making inferences is a powerful way for students to deepen their comprehension of a text. Students will use this worksheet to make inferences about whom Daisy actually loves—Tom or Gatsby or neither. For each piece of textual evidence provided, students will record their inferences as to what the details reveal about Daisy's true feelings. They will then use these inferences to make a determination about whom Daisy loves.

RL.11-12.1 Cite strong and thorough textual evidence to support analysis of what the text says explicitly as well as inferences drawn from the text, including determining where the text leaves matters uncertain.

Whom Does Daisy Love?

While *The Great Gatsby* largely focuses on Gatsby's love for Daisy, by the end of the novel, readers are left unclear on whether Daisy loves him or Tom—or if she truly loves either of them at all. As Daisy never states her true feelings, we must make inferences, or educated guesses, about whom she actually loves.

Read each piece of evidence from the text, and write an inference about what this evidence reveals about Daisy's true feelings.

Evidence	Inference
Daisy married Tom Buchanan.	She may have felt some affection for him at some point but may have mainly been attracted to his wealth and status.
Jordan tells Nick that the night before Daisy married Tom, Daisy cried.	
Daisy and Gatsby begin an affair.	
At the hotel in New York, Daisy cannot say she never loved Tom, as Gatsby urges her to do.	
Daisy hits Myrtle Wilson while driving Gatsby's car and lets Gatsby take the blame for it.	
Daisy leaves East Egg with Tom before Gatsby's funeral.	

Use your inferences above to answer the following question: Do you think Daisy was in love with Tom, Gatsby, or neither of them?

*sparkteach   37

Timeline: Putting Events in Order

Overview

Complex text structures—in particular, structures in which events are revealed out of chronological order—can confuse a reader, weakening comprehension. Students will use this worksheet to put events presented by Nick in *The Great Gatsby* in chronological order to better understand the novel and to draw conclusions about how the structure affects the reader. Hand out the worksheet after students have finished the novel. As a class, discuss how learning of the events as Nick learns of them has a different effect than if the events had been revealed in chronological order.

Answer Key

Nick's Order of Events	Chronological Order
1. Nick moves to Long Island.	4
2. Nick meets Gatsby at one of Gatsby's parties.	5
3. Gatsby and Daisy have a relationship before she is married.	2
4. Nick invites Daisy to his house to reunite with Gatsby.	6
5. James Gatz changed his name to Jay Gatsby.	1
6. A yellow car hits and kills Myrtle Wilson.	8
7. Daisy decides to drive Gatsby's car home from New York.	7
8. Gatsby travels to Louisville to find Daisy only to discover that she is married to Tom.	3
9. George Wilson shoots Gatsby and then himself.	9

RL.11-12.5 Analyze how an author's choices concerning how to structure specific parts of a text (e.g., the choice of where to begin or end a story, the choice to provide a comedic or tragic resolution) contribute to its overall structure and meaning as well as its aesthetic impact.

Timeline: Putting Events in Order

Although Nick claims to be recounting past events, he describes them in the order he learns of them, not in strictly chronological order.

First, read the text's major events in the order Nick learns of them. Next, write the events in chronological order on the second timeline. How do the differences in the order of events affect the reader's experience of the novel?

Nick's Order of Events

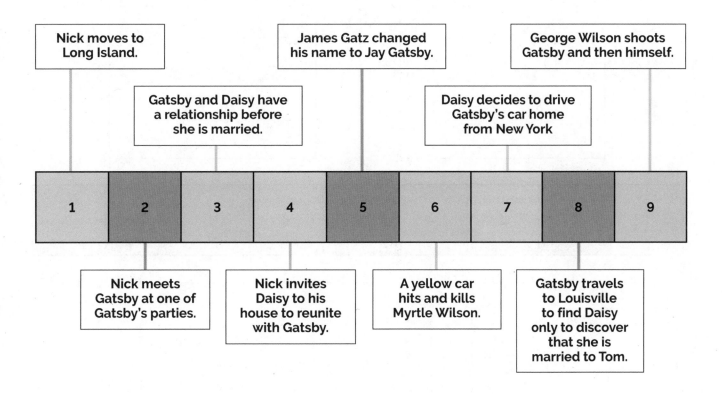

Chronological Order

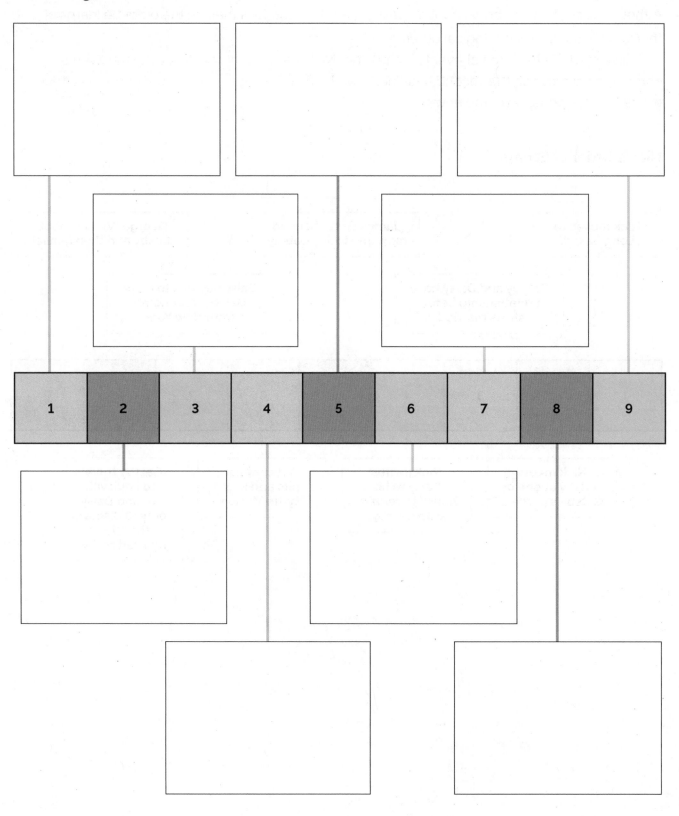

Driving Questions

Driving Questions	Initial Answer	Final Answer
What does the American Dream mean to each character in the novel?	Text evidence:	Text evidence:
How do various characters in the novel try to achieve the American Dream?	Text evidence:	Text evidence:
How is Gatsby's love for Daisy a metaphor for the American Dream?	Text evidence:	Text evidence:
How has the country changed since the days of Gatsby and Nick?	Text evidence:	Text evidence:

Driving Questions	Initial Answer	Final Answer
What is each character's motivation for achieving the American Dream?	Text evidence:	Text evidence:
Has Gatsby achieved the American Dream before the end of the novel?	Text evidence:	Text evidence:
How is the green light on Daisy's dock relevant to the American Dream?	Text evidence:	Text evidence:

Character	Does the character exhibit signs of greed?	What motivates the character's greed?
Jay Gatsby	Yes. Jay has an enormous house and likes to show off his wealth.	his love for Daisy
Nick Carraway		
Daisy Buchanan		
Tom Buchanan		
Jordan Baker		
Myrtle Wilson		
George Wilson		

RL.11-12.2 Determine two or more themes or central ideas of a text and analyze their development over the course of the text, including how they interact and build on one another to produce a complex account; provide an objective summary of the text.

PART 4
Postmortem

After the unit, use the following Rubric for Student Assessment to assess your students' learning and the Student and Teacher Reflection worksheets to capture your experience with the Lesson Plans.

Rubric for Student Assessment

Overview

Using a rubric can help you assess students' learning more accurately and more consistently. Giving the rubric to your students before they begin a task that will be assessed also makes your expectations clear and encourages students to take responsibility for their own learning and success on an assignment. This rubric can be used across multiple midpoint activities and final projects to assess students' learning and understanding. You can also edit a version of the rubric to tailor it to specific learning goals you have for your classes.

Rubric for Student Assessment

Area of Performance	4	3	2	1
Content development	Work clearly and thoroughly addresses the prompt. All details/ideas support the main topic. Ideas are original, creative, and supported by numerous concrete details from the text.	Work mostly addresses the prompt. Most details/ideas support the main topic. A few concrete details from the text are provided.	Work doesn't stay on target and/or doesn't follow the prompt. Only a few supporting details are provided.	Work doesn't stay on target or follow the prompt. Ideas are confusing. Details are irrelevant or missing.
Organization	Details are presented in a logical and meaningful order. Essays or presentations include a clear introduction, body, and conclusion. Statements reflect critical thinking skills. Appropriate transitions are used to connect ideas.	Most details are presented in a logical order and are related to the main topic. The writing is clear, but the introduction, body, or conclusion needs strengthening.	Many details are presented in an illogical order or are unrelated to the main topic. The writing lacks a clear introduction, well-organized body, or a strong conclusion.	Details and ideas are poorly organized and unrelated to main topic.
Language and style	Writing or spoken language is smooth, coherent, and stays on topic. Sentence structure varies. Strong verbs and descriptive details and language clarify and strengthen ideas.	Writing or spoken language stays on topic but sentence structure doesn't vary. Some descriptive details are used to clarify ideas.	Some writing or spoken language doesn't flow and/or lacks creativity. Some language unrelated to or inappropriate for the main topic is used.	Writing or spoken language is confusing. Incomplete or run-on sentences are used. Many terms used are unrelated to or inappropriate for the main topic.

Area of Performance	4	3	2	1
Mechanics (when applicable)	All grammar and punctuation is correct. The writing is free of spelling errors.	The writing is mostly free of grammatical, mechanical, and spelling errors.	Writing contains several grammatical, punctuation, and spelling errors.	The writing contains numerous errors that make it difficult to understand.
Collaboration (when applicable)	Student played a valuable role in group work. Student worked well with others, listened respectfully to others' ideas, and resolved any challenges in an appropriate manner.	Student played an important role in group work but could have been more open to others' ideas and/or could have resolved challenges in a more constructive manner.	Student did minimal work in his/her group. Student ignored group challenges or left challenges unresolved.	Student didn't do her/his fair share of work. Student did not engage in the group task.
Research (when applicable)	Multiple, reliable sources were used to gather information. All sources are properly cited or credited.	Some research was done to complete the task. Not all sources are cited or some citations are incomplete.	Little or no research was done to gather necessary information. No sources are cited.	No research was done.

Student and Teacher Reflection Worksheets

Overview

A reflective practice helps you continue to develop new and engaging teaching strategies that meet the needs of all students in your class. Tracking successes as well as challenges throughout a unit of study also decreases planning time for future classes and helps you tailor your lessons to improve each time you teach them. Use this worksheet to reflect on a Real-Life Lens Lesson you have taught and record what was successful and what you would change when you teach the material again. Make notes on interesting ideas you added to the Lens Lesson or thoughts your students had that inspired you along the way.

Student Reflection Worksheet

1. How did reading the text through the lens of the American Dream affect your engagement with and understanding of this text?

   _____

   _____

   _____

2. What difficulties did you encounter with this text, and how did you address them?

   _____

   _____

   _____

3. Consider the Real-Life Links you encountered at the beginning of the lesson. Which resources did you find the most interesting? Why?

   _____

   _____

4. How effective were the Driving Questions in guiding you to a deeper understanding of the text?

   _____

   _____

   _____

5. Describe one challenge you faced while working on an activity or project and how you overcame it.

   _____

   _____

   _____

6. What new insight or skill did you take away from this lesson?

   _____

   _____

   _____

Teacher Reflection Worksheet

1. How did the lens applied in this lesson affect student engagement and comprehension?

   _____

   _____

   _____

2. How did students respond to the Real-Life Links? Did some resources spark more interest than others?

   _____

   _____

   _____

3. Did you or any of your students come up with additional Driving Questions? If so, record them here to use the next time you teach this lesson.

   _____

   _____

4. Which activities inspired students the most?

   _____

   _____

   _____

5. What difficulties did students encounter, how did you address them, and were your interventions successful?

   _____

   _____

   _____

6. Were there worksheets, activities, or projects that you will revise the next time you present this lesson? If so, what changes will you make?

   _____

   _____

   _____